Citizenship

By Tracy Vonder Brink

Table of Contents

A Starfish Book

SEAHORSE
PUBLISHING

Teaching Tips for Caregivers:

As a caregiver, you can help your child succeed in school by giving them a strong foundation in language and literacy skills and a desire to learn to read.

This book helps children grow by letting them practice reading skills.

Reading for pleasure and interest will help your child to develop reading skills and will give your child the opportunity to practice these skills in meaningful ways.

- Encourage your child to read on her own at home
- Encourage your child to practice reading aloud
- Encourage activities that require reading
- Establish a reading time
- Talk with your child
- Give your child writing materials

Teaching Tips for Teachers:

Research shows that one of the best ways for students to learn a new topic is to read about it.

Before Reading

- Read the "Words to Know" and discuss the meaning of each word.
- Read the back cover to see what the book is about.

During Reading

- When a student gets to a word that is unknown, ask them to look at the rest of the sentence to find clues to help with the meaning of the unknown word.
- Ask the student to write down any pages of the book that was confusing to them.

After Reading

- Discuss the main idea of the book.
- Ask students to give one detail that they learned in the book by showing a text dependent answer from the book.

Citizenship

A citizen is a member of a country.

U.S. citizens are also known as Americans.

All people born in the United States are its citizens.

Children of Americans are also U.S. citizens.

This is true even if they are born in another country.

Immigrants are people from other countries who move to the U.S.

They may choose to become U.S. citizens.

They must follow steps to do so.

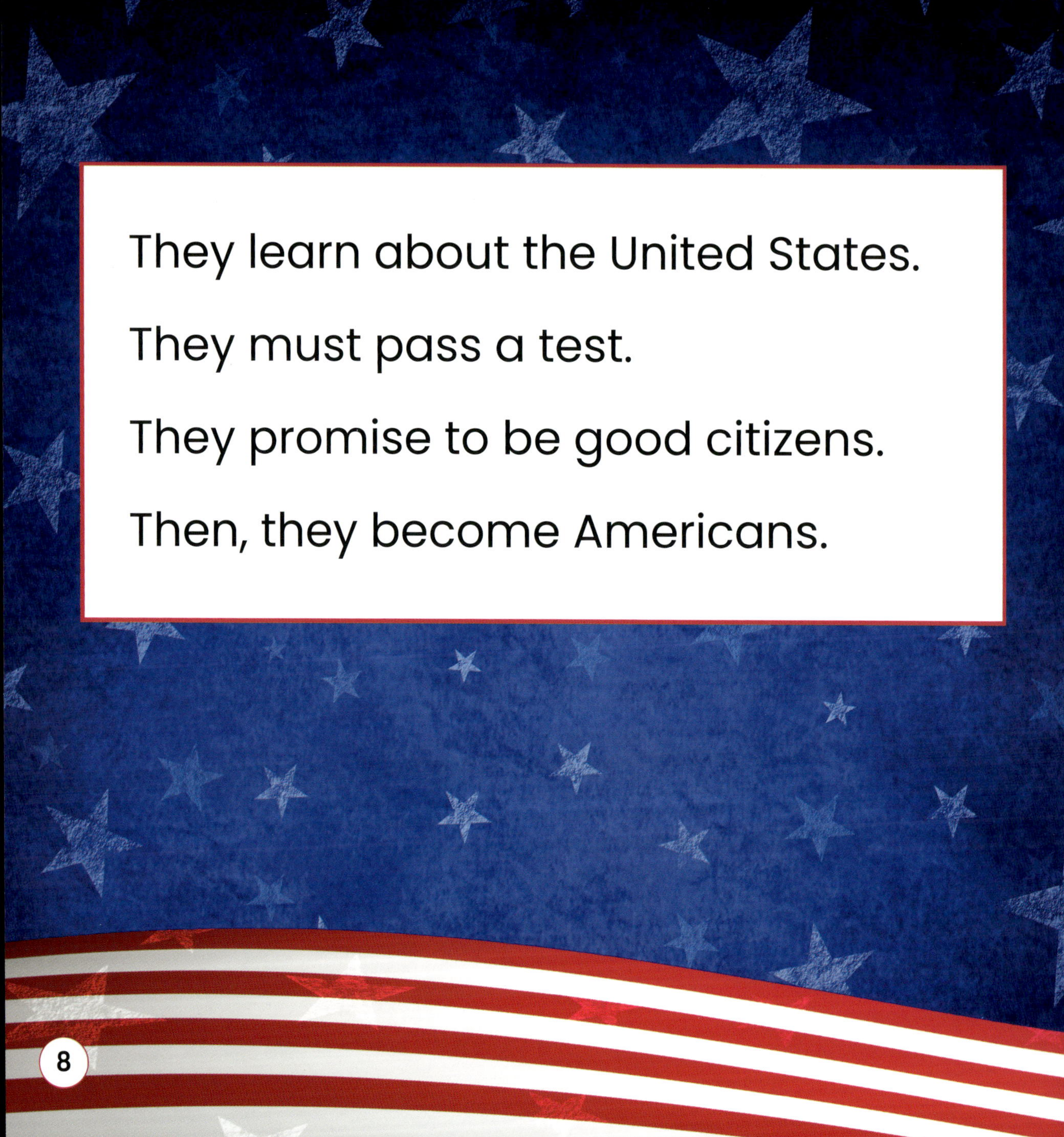

They learn about the United States.

They must pass a test.

They promise to be good citizens.

Then, they become Americans.

Americans have **rights**.

They can **vote**.

People who are not citizens cannot vote.

Americans vote for the president and other leaders.

Some jobs require workers to be citizens.

Only Americans may be elected as leaders.

Only people born in the United States may become president.

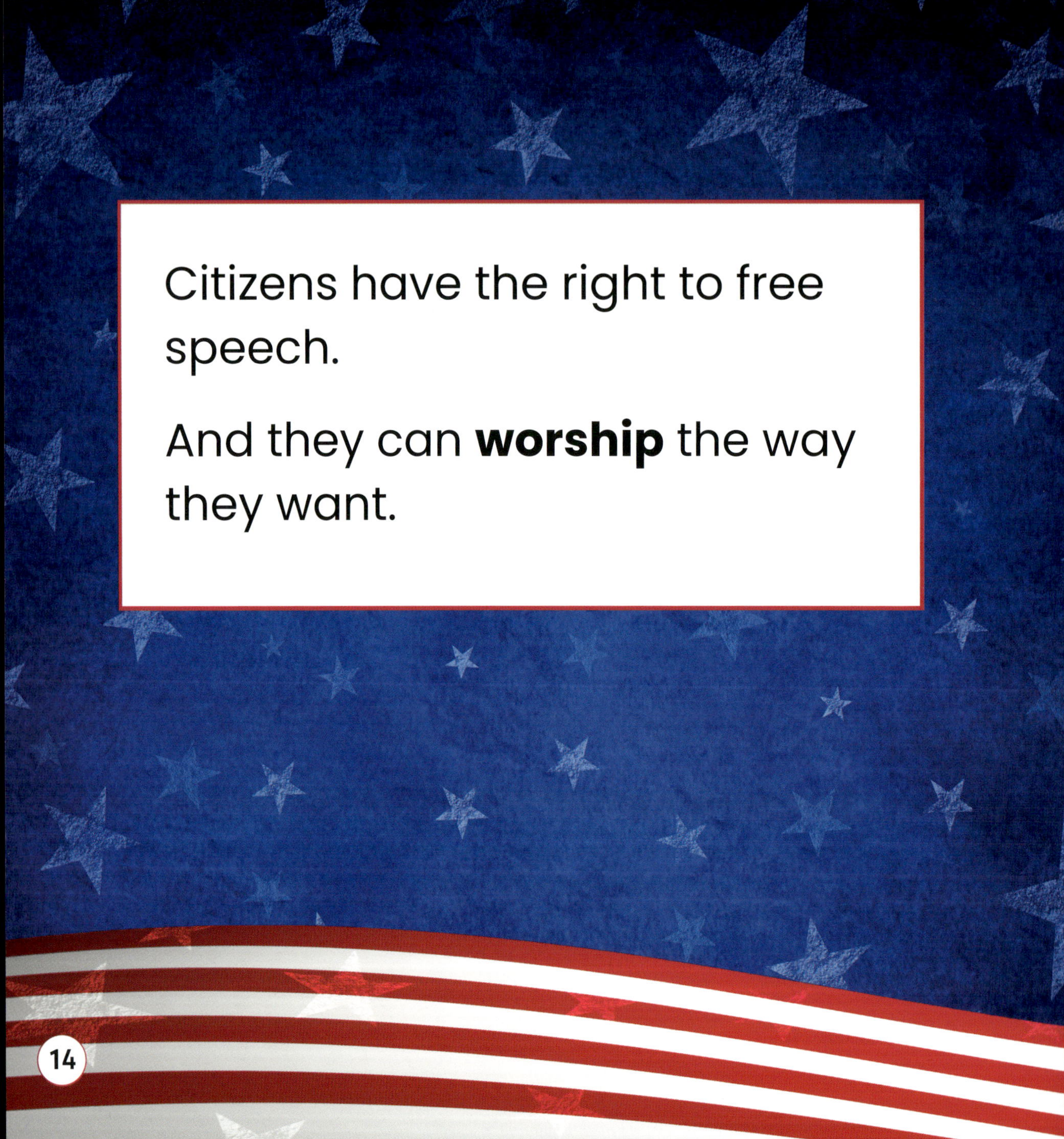

Citizens have the right to free speech.

And they can **worship** the way they want.

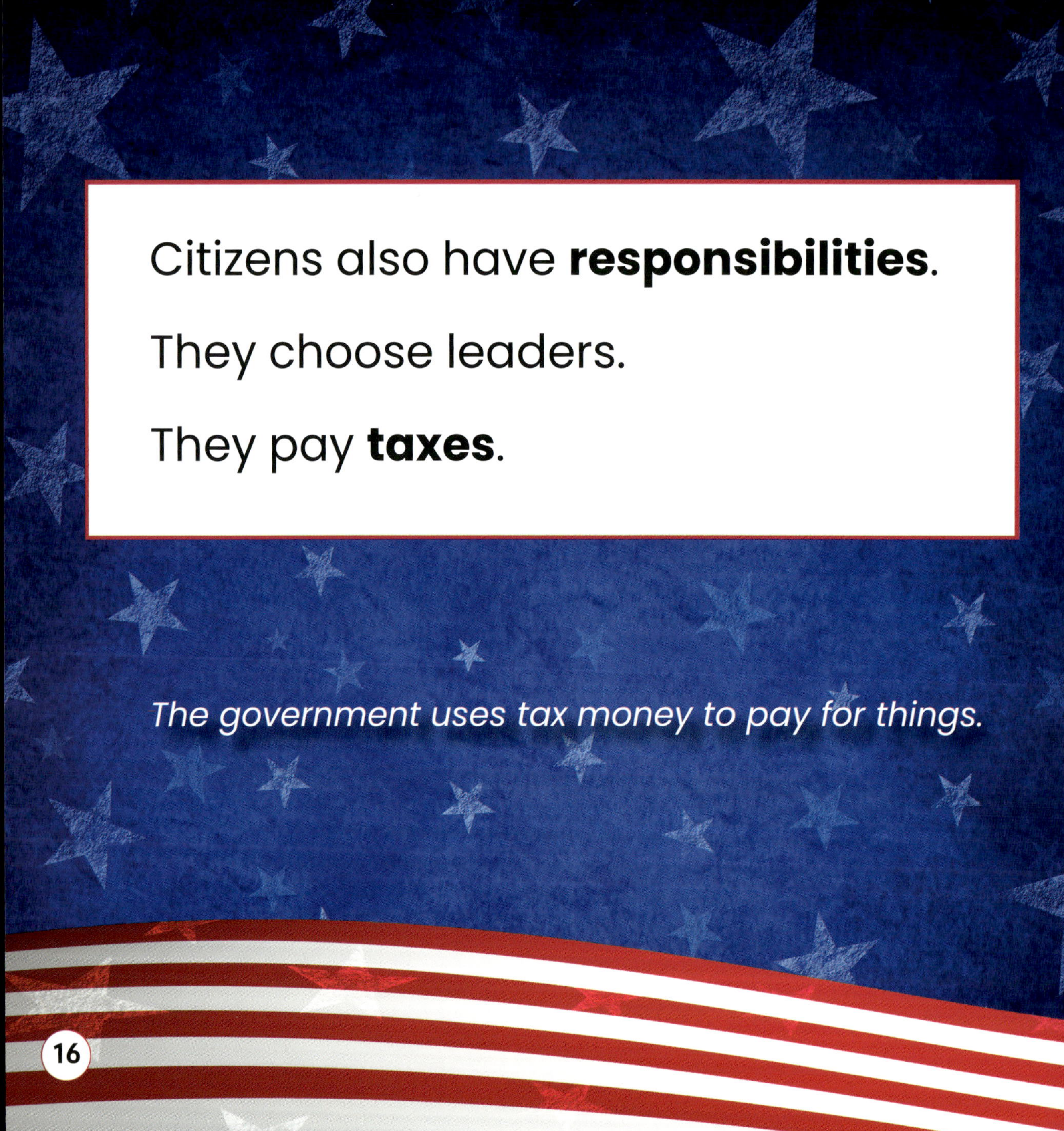

Citizens also have **responsibilities**.

They choose leaders.

They pay **taxes**.

The government uses tax money to pay for things.

040 Department of the Treasury—Internal Revenue Service
U.S. Individual Income Tax R

year Jan. 1–Dec. 31, 2013, or other tax year beginning

irst name and initial | Last name

oint return, spouse's first name and initial | Last name

me address (number and street). If you have a P.O. box, see ins

ty, town or post office, state, and ZIP code. If you have a foreign addr

Foreign country name

Filing Status

k only one

1 ☐ Single

2 ☐ Married filing jointly (ev

3 ☐ Married filing separate
and full name here. ▶

Citizens obey laws.

They take care of each other.

They help take care of their community.

VOLUNTEER

They also work to make their community a better place to live.

A country needs good citizens.

Words to Know

immigrants (IH-muh-grunts): people who come to a different country to make a new home

responsibilities (ruh-spawn-suh-BI-luh-tees): things people are expected to do

rights (rites): things a person is allowed to do under the law

taxes (TAK-suz): money that people pay to the government

vote (voht): to make a choice for or against someone or something

worship (WUR-shup): to take part in a religious service

Index

Comprehension Questions

1. What are some rights American citizens have?
   a. the right to vote
   b. the right to worship the way they want
   c. both A and B

2. Who can become a leader in America?
   a. immigrants
   b. military members only
   c. American citizens

3. What is a citizen?
   a. a member of a country
   b. a member of a team
   c. a member of a club

4. **True or False:** People who are not citizens can vote.

5. **True or False:** Citizens must pay taxes.

Answers
1. c 2. c 3. a 4. False 5. True

About the Author

Tracy Vonder Brink enjoys learning about the United States. She is an American. Tracy lives in Cincinnati with her husband, two daughters, and two rescue dogs.

Written by: Tracy Vonder Brink
Design by: Kathy Walsh
Editor: Kim Thompson

Photographs/Shutterstock: Cover ©topseller: Cover, Pg 1 ©Tuari Media, ©Lightspring, ©Vertes Edmond Mihai: Pg 4-21 ©Lightspring: Pg 3 ©Monkey Business Images: Pg 5 ©Zurijeta: Pg 7 ©Diego G Diaz: Pg 9 ©Kim Kelley-Wagner: Pg 11 ©vesperstock: Pg 13 ©Sean Locke Photography: Pg 15 ©Chanyanuch Wannasinlapin: Pg 17 ©Eastside Cindy: Pg 19 ©Dmytro Zinkevych: Pg 20 ©Rawpixel.com

Library of Congress PCN Data
Citizenship / Tracy Vonder Brink
Civic Readiness
ISBN 978-1-63897-090-3 (hard cover)
ISBN 978-1-63897-176-4 (paperback)
ISBN 978-1-63897-262-4 (EPUB)
ISBN 978-1-63897-348-5 (eBook)
Library of Congress Control Number: 2021945205

Printed in the United States of America.

Seahorse Publishing Company
www.seahorsepub.com

Published in the United States
Seahorse Publishing
PO Box 771325
Coral Springs, FL 33077